Foreword

Everything I have written in times of sorrow, in woe, in times of love and ecstasy; a collection of (nearly) all my poems from the year of 2019 (and additions from 2018). This was a period of great confusion for me and thus many of what you are about to read may be incoherent; especially since the large majority are inspired by a concoction of drugs, mental illness, heartbreak, and self-loathing.

There are a fair few love poems in this work, or so I feel, this was for me a time to awaken and realise my value; learn a few lessons. I had given my heart to someone for it to be ripped out of my chest time and time again.

In and out of melancholy, love, toxicity, and sobriety the following poems are the expression of my soul clawing its way to this plain of reality.

With love;

Jonny Cosmo...

Acknowledgements

Thank you to those who hurt me for inspiring me to write and giving me the anguish deep enough to become who I am today.

A thank you also goes out to those who have supported me, I wouldn't be here without you.

Finally a special thanks to my illustrator Edie, you've supported me since day and into the tomorrow. I appreciate you greatly.

00:11 30/09/19

A. D. H. D.

Just four letters but they change how you think of me

Once bright, eccentric, charismatic

Now you question my sanity

Now you look at me as if to see a spanner in the works

As if me an individual, different than you, from birth, in life, in experience, in thought - as is everyone, even most likely differently taught

But four letters change all of that in a second and the exact thing that

beforehand made you curious to know me now makes you

uncomfortable because you wonder how they control me

What pills for my ills do I need to be subdued?

How about just a hammer and chisel up my nose, clink, and you can bare me, am I scary?

See it's odd to think that the exact tick that distracts my attention is the exact thing that also heightens my perception... I over think...

See because when I told you just four letters, your left eye twitched, you retracted your gullet, your brow raised-fell? I couldn't tell because in that millisecond you caught it and then you fought the urge to tilt up your head and look down your nose at me; but you did, I saw it, by the minimal degree your face showed a

decree of what you now think of me. But I'm used to it, it's hard to

understand what's going on
upstairs in someone else's psych
land, but every hand is still flesh
and bone.

A. D. H. D.

Sometimes it makes work hard,
doing work, finding work, keeping
work, finding work again again
again again again again again, I
need a sick day please, a chill day,
a free from stress day, because it's
not easy to be me and for you I
have to be this thing that beeps,
submits, smiles.

DECLARE YOUR MENTAL HEALTH

why so you can discriminate under
the table against my will because
you think I'm less able, unless PR
said you need a token in the
workplace.

A. D. H. D.

That's what they call it anyway, this one thing, my first diagnosis but I could tell you I'm also depressed and anxious, apparently due to stress from having ADHD but how does that mean my problems are any smaller. How bout we add dyspraxia in there, hey I'm epileptic too but just by adding to this list you now can't resist to again and again change your view of me with each letter, you might think that I'm better off dosed, of locked up. You might feel empathy or are you sure it's not sympathy, please do not pity me can't you see for all its worth we are stood in the same room. None of this makes me better. If it makes you then by all means follow through with your reactionary thought but a book is far better than its blurb.

Astounding. Couldn't wait to read the next page. Truly one of a kind.

1/5 went off on tangents a lot couldn't follow.

A. D. H. D

We're all different. Even as newborn infants.

Can't we just wait a little longer, read more than the cover, give at least the first page a chance, before we put the book back down judged at a glance.

A. D. H. Me.

A. D. H. We.

In a world where nobody can look up from their phone screens, constantly flicking through images, messages, articles and games. To resort back to our dwellings, or sitting with the family or friends, to again stare back at our screens,

with another screen for background stimulation, because silence has become so unbearable.

Only a maniac would tell a child,
deficit of attention with energy and
determination to match a jet engine
has a disorder.

19:26 06/10/19
Love affliction/addiction

See I thought maybe I was only ever happy with the taste of you on my lips

Your breath
in my lungs

Your acidic
nature
upsetting my
stomach

But to
witness an autumnal sunset with a clear mind on a clear day

That is what for I sleep so I may wake

I felt safe with you in my hand, my pocket, my bag

Although sometimes we had obscure looks from the public it didn't matter, we had each other

Your smell would linger on my clothes

Then I realised what it was to be free and that in fact the only thing holding anything back or stopping me was me

I used to close my eyes and I'd smile because for the first time in what felt like a while I felt alright

I was happy of sorts as if in a dream I never wanted to wake up from my reality was what you gave me

At night you helped me sleep
soundly I didn't dream I didn't need
to because I had you, you were all
my dreams awake

But in the morning you were
scarce, and I would get scared in
case I never found you

Again

Of course, I'd always find you again,
on the streets or with friends there
was never an end to the love and
the loss

You made me feel strong

But then you were gone

You made me feel happy

But in my lows I got angsty

Now I am without you and its true I
don't feel like I did with you, I'm
scared, I'm sad, I'm alone

But tomorrow is another day and
for the sunrise, sunset I await. For
the first time in a while to see with
sober eyes, sober mind, sober not
somber smile.

23/11/2019 Somewhere around midnight, dark cloud

Sometimes I'm not okay

But in the end it doesn't matter tomorrow's another day

and the next it's the same

back and around endlessly circling rebound

Laugh like a clown do you see a frown when I'm lost

Spaced away, I wish all day every day, because it's the only way I find that I escape

It always returns...

<u>25/10/19 18:26 Company</u>

Nobody wants your company

Unless you are happy

But what if you struggle being happy

Nobody wants your company

Lottery

It's like I never learnt to swim
because I was always given
armbands

Now whenever I'm in water I
feel like I'm drowning

I should have learnt to swim

Life is pay to win

But when someone pays for
you

How can you learn anythin'

<u>24/10/19 14:05</u> **Proverb**

Life is alike standing in a slow-moving stream, looking back, or looking forward it is clear to see movement in shimmer and mirage.

Looking at your feet movement is only clear on the ripples you make.

24/10/19 13:49 VALHALLA

Is a warrior who dies in battle more victorious than one that doesn't fall

It maybe so but the warrior who comes home lives to fight another battle

In the midst of darkness, in red, in war.

Dying in the name of grace may seem courageous

But victorious are the survivors who fight to come home.

24/10/19 13:58 Southstack

Waves crash

Upon rocks cracked

A lighthouse stands pronounced

A beacon for ships passed

The ocean shouts

Cliffs collapse

The immense power elapsed

The cliffs wave

And the ocean cracks

Boulders stack

Flowers grip to that

Layers upon layers of time

Twisted contorted against nature's brace

Timeless cliff face

Weathered with age

Built upon another age

A written story without a page.

23/10/19 21:20 Poser

People might think I'm fake

Because I am oh too real

They'd rather be fed on a plate

Full of pleasing lies for a meal

Do you want to hear the truth?

Or do you want to stay
ignorant?

From you're reality aloof

Deception malignant

23/10/19 16:41 Today

Today's not a sad day

It's a I've had many before day

It's a sit in the backseat day

It's I slept in till 3 day

It's a can't get dressed day

It's I don't want to eat day

It's can I just go back to sleep day

It's I don't know day

It's I don't want day

It's I've got shit to do today

Some days they're just the same in the way that my brain seems to melt away

I can't feel can't think can't speak
all I want is to be asleep I'm weak

It's like cleaning my teeth is a
conversation one that I didn't
expect to have but I'm here all the
same someone else is making my
decisions I've never made my own I
guess I've just done what was
necessary

The only texts I get out the blue is
bill's is doctors is dealer's never hey
how are you because you know I'll
be blue so what's the point in
asking

I'm just doing to do I have no
reason to I have nothing to do get
dressed grab my phone grab my
headphones head out hit the town
wonder round looking for a feeling

20/10/19 23:56 Hard

There's more lessons to learn from losing

In winning you might find you are abusing

Choosing the path to most likely succeed

Will end in most likely catastrophe

Being at the bottom means the only way is up

To stay at the top you will need more than luck

Chuck aside lowly ego

Hold onto desire to evolve

Short paths make for fast journeys

Long paths however provide us with learning

My sister, for her 21st Birthday

My sister, what can I say about how I feel.

She's like a blister on the bottom of my heel.

At uni I miss her yeah the loss is real.

But it's okay.

Because one day.

She'll be serving this country not unlike a soldier on the battlefield.

Needles for bullets.

Blood for blood.

Life for war.

I know you'll do good.

Trivialities aside all in all.

This is your birthday not works beckoning call.

For now you are a woman.

All grown and going on.
You'll do great things.

A vouch from me, your friends and home.

I hope you have a lovely day, or week, or month.

I'm kidding she's not a princess.

She's a soldier in a tunic uniform.

So dance a jig and swig ya drink.

Raise a glass for my blister.

And hope tonight your heels don't give you a sister.

19/10/19 00:05 Lesson of expression

My phone autocorrected

Expression to depression

Oh how that is a lesson

If I seek happiness

Why don't I preach it

Instead I speak my woes

And your happiness I leach it

See how can I spread love

If all I say is my sorrow

Who wants to know

Your smile I borrow

How can we

Speak of good times

If all we do is commit

Conversational crime

18/10/19 23:57 Beans

As humans we live within our
means

At one point that meant in trees

Now we swing from post to partner

Should I be a banker or a gardener?

As humans we live within our
means

And this means some of us live
alike Diogenes

The streets are a cold dark place

But here you'll find high spirits,
perseverance, and grace

See as humans we live within our
means

And sometimes that is we live to
please

New shoes new phone new everything

See I'm good I'm happy check my bling

See as humans we live within our means

Lest we forget we're no happier than monkeys in trees

Ode to Sartre

I'd rather die on my feet,

Than live on my knees.

Rather die free,

Than live as a thing.

I'd rather die cold and hungry,

Than live warm in chains.

I'd rather die on my feet,

Than live by your hands.
I am a human being.

18/10/19 22:07 Waste

I tried to spend a day
relaxing and wasting

But I couldn't relax just
wasted

Now there's hours of my life
I'll never seen again

And I spent them coming to
no ends

16/10/19 15:39 Thug

Drugs tend to make a mug
before they make a thug sit like
a slug make your own grave
dug bottle bag chug just give
you more to lug than you
already should

15/10/19 Liv

I'm happy now he misses me

I missed him for the whole
relationship

Where was he when I was there

I was there when he wasn't here

He came home to my warmth

His cold came with and swarmed

I would sit for him and wait

He would always stay out late

Too tired for me to give comfort

I kept doing what I should

He didn't see what he had

I'm now gone and I am glad

14/10/19 12:18 World mental health day

Today is world mental health day
So now you can all pretend you're not a cunt day
Where's your empathy when it isn't trendy
I'm sorry to be so bleak but at the peak of this subject dwells those who speak ill of the ill.
Fuck off you fucking fuck - you're a cunt - if you don't know how to show kindness without want.
I speak from experience when I say it isn't easy, what was harder was trying to take my own life we humans are very resilient.
So don't turn around and chat about that if you're sad to reach out
To you.
Where were you when your friend felt blue.
Or green, or red or yellow too.
Mental health isn't just anxiety or depression.
It's also the fact men can't use emotive expression

It's women being objectified for the body
they're born in
It's children being ridiculed for their
status, genetics or mistakes
Mental health is saying no when you
don't want
Mental health is looking after you first
before your own
Mental health is swimming at high tide
Mental health should never be drowning
cold, alone in the dark

So don't wait for anyone, to reach out to
you, not your friends or family or even
strangers at the bus stop.

Ask people how they are and mean when
you say it, listen to their problems, hug
them, help them
Don't brush anything away, like all it is,
is dust

We are not our bodies, but we are our
psyches.

I am mental
Health everyday

14/10/19 12:12
Appointment

So you've come to address your mental health

Of course this isn't you reaching out for help

This is just a chat to see what list we can put you on

Oh you're not suicidal today? No worries how does 6-12 months sound

It says here you've been to us before, strange that quick fix didn't fix shit but I bet this isn't a chore

Let's send you back to where you've already been

I'd recommend a psychological route unfortunately due to underfunding we don't have one in

In fact we don't have them in Lancashire for the NHS because nobody can pay them

It's alright find a private psychiatrist who gets off on dosing you up, your prescription will pay for their jaguar oh how empathetic they must be

The state of North Western mental health never mind just the health service - nurses pushed to the end of their tether,

consultants paid bags

sympathy never

Behold the North West, joblessness and poverty rife

Why spend more money on our health service

When we're the soonest to die

12/10/19 17:31 Chemicals

Keep getting told depression
damages your brain but that's
the reason I refrain from taking
chemicals that a man choked
by a tie tells me I need incase I
might die, side effects include
wanting to die so why oh why
the fuck oh right yeah of
course my emotions are out of
control because I just feel
things in whole there's no
partial in passion so my life
just feels tragic even when it's
not

11/10/19 22:06 Whether

Born in 97

Born raised lived in Preston

One day just another look
outside to see clouds grey

Be reet I say

If anything it'll just be a drizzle

It was not just a drizzle

09/10/19 21:43 Education

Cram repeat cram repeat cram repeat here's a degree

Is anyone really learning or are we just regurgitating as opposed to thinking on our feet

Dropped in the deep at 18

After school is all done, you learn more through turmoil and war than you do the safety and warmth of a classroom

This is known. This is fact and yet here we are again year after year pushing pupils to achieve higher test scores as if you can compare a brain and all its majesty to a number or letter

09/10/19 21:23 Slow change

Rather than no change

Do you have any spare change

Less shocking than fast change

Easier than a mood change

Not as healthy as food change

Make something from your loose change

Need it if we're ever gonna have a role change

Tectonic movements makes a pole change

Meditation over years for a soul change

Jobseekers universal credit dole change

All of this together makes the whole change

Let's make the world change

09/10/19 16:09 Enough time

I've realised that there are enough hours in the day.

When your mind isn't dulled from substance and you don't sleep the light away.

Imagine how many thoughts you have in 600 seconds without any distraction, numbing or ailment.

That's 10 minutes, 10 minutes is 600 seconds.

Now my mind is clearer I can use that 10 minutes as if it was eternity.

At one point it felt as if there wasn't enough time in the day.

Now I wish they were shorter so I wasn't as busy and in bed sooner.

Life is as short as the day is long. It just depends how much you spend it idle or forlorn.

06/10/19 19:26 Harmony

Out of the dark and into the light

Despite the rattle I hear inside my mind

Opaque is the lens over the window to the soul

The seat of which upon "I" sit, to think is to know

Brace yourself for these are words of truth

The holy and be it the damned may think this obtuse

But to fight the right and fear the left

To fear the dark and seek the light

Takes away from you that is that makes you whole

Choice makes us human you already know

To ascribe good is to confuse what is evil

To be sinister is to forget beneval

Balance is key to all things alive

From stars to atoms to yin and yang

Harmony comes from equal sides

See I am not asking for you to be or live in grey

Simply match selfless with a bit of selfish per day

A strong fist and a soft touch

Compassion matches anger

Charity to greed

Whatever it is to be human, truly to know one must be absolutely free

06/10/19 19:26 Realise

Same name, same game different day you're in a daze from too much haze if you think it's gonna get better

If you're still feeling wetter hoping for better weather but your minds wrapped in latex and leather could you balance your heart to a feather I think not

But if you're feeling hot alike you've lost the plot it can't be washed down with a shot in fact you're better off looking at the clock and remembering your time here is limited

Eliminate anyone anything who tries to state you've got time to waste and not that there's in fact a

number to your days here present
or be it alive

Peace of mind, live in the hive
dance sing and jive pass the time
but don't let yourself fade away.

Live the now like it's all you have
because it is at the end of the day,
even the material can last longer,
longer than your life. We're all dust.

In the back of a cosmic truck, we're
just floating down a galactic river,
so ditch the triv n start to see
things for the now n hither.

06/10/19 19:26 Shadow

I'm not afraid of the dark

The dark is afraid of me

See what was lurking under my bed

Is far less than the monsters hiding
inside my head

Ghosts and ghoulies

Nothing to the imagination of we

Or better yet who we are
underneath

"These meddling kids" I said as I
took off my mask

But again another face

And another, another again

Until finally

I am nothing but a shadow of my own reflection

That stands tall in the sun's coronation

There's no monsters with fangs and long claws

There is men with hot blood and dirty paws

There are suit's wearing bodies

Smiles that cast out a sense of security underneath razorblade teeth waiting till your gaze is away

See I look into my shadow and accept its less narrow now that I see the monster in the mirror

I'm not afraid of the dark

The dark is afraid of me

05/10/19 01:23 Got out

I had to get out and I did.

The fact that the potential mother of my future kids made me want to slit my wrists, but I never did.

In fact, I had to fight blades from between her fingers and the sight of blood in the bathtub still lingers in my mind every time I close my eyes I think I might be traumatised but of course I'm a man it doesn't affect me.

If I shout the police are round then I'm out in the back of a van because I asked who that man was in your bedroom.

If you shout, I couldn't get out, you'd give me a clout even when I was bleeding having had to fight for you. What could I do. Keys were hid, doors locked, police round I'm out, back of a van, thank you for taking me away.

I couldn't stay with someone who just stood in my way when I was trying to build a road, we could both walk on.

I wish you'd leave my head, you told me you'd rather I was dead, multiple times, multiple times you shared OUR bed. And I was stupid enough to look past it instead. I stayed until I was completely broken.

When I was 1 maybe 2 I learnt to walk.

At 16 I almost lost a leg and I had to relearn to walk. I taught myself.

I'm 22 and because of you, I feel I haven't found my feet again. I will walk again. One foot in front of the other. Then I can run. I will bask in the sun.

On the road that I built for myself.

I had to get out.   I. did.

03/10/19 16:24
SUPERFICIAL

Different just like YOUR different

Hollow people with painted faces

No soul
to fill
the
spaces

Beasts
of
desire

A smile
for hire

Substances to give your life
substance

Empty promises and broken
silences

True charity is rare, judged by the clothes you wear

Tell me how you see a beautiful soul if beauty is only skin deep

Your bedsheets Egyptian silk, in a dirty sack on the streets a man sleeps

Idle minds and active digits

Keep your prodigy child distracted with a spinner fidget

Good people with no morals

But I was drunk it's fine no quarrel

Lie to others don't tell the truth

Keep your secrets under roof

Like to speak but never listen

Everyone is a rose all I see is thistles

Rather not let go at fear of being alone

Sell your ass so your life can pass right before your eyes

Give years to your television, reality TV isn't fiction

Tell me Nobel prize winners, tell me chart music fillers, tell me about celebs personal lives, forget whatever drives you to do the impossible.

As a child have dreams, grow up because they're not plausible.

Tell me what scares you tell me about your fears

Less of the dark or death more people's jests and jeers.

Have a belief have an opinion.

Fall under scrutiny's dominion.

Don't even speak if you have a religion.

Hate falls like rain.

From love comes pain.

Read magazines stay skinny.

But.

Read books and then you're winning.

Stay true be you.

Stand out of the crowd, stand proud.

Neither wolves nor shepherds sleep at the feet of sheep.

Meditate don't procrastinate.

Shop for charity I promise you'll gain more clarity

Wait and save, don't spend and slave.

Feed your soul not your appetite

In moderation we claim true gratification

Stay off social media you'll just get greedier in fact social marketing is a better tool for business.

Your business is your own, remember that if you feel alone.

Speak to be known not to be heard, hold your tongue if its a filler word.

Smile brighter than the sunrise

And breathe in a sunset

I'm still learning I'll admit to that

But get out the race fast it's full of rats

Answer to you and who is your integrity

Why are we even listening to paper-thin blow-up-doll celebrities?

Trust scientists, listen to priests, Heck even listen to that dirty poor man sitting on the street.

Everyone you meet

Is another book

You just have to ask their story.

Face value might as well behead
that mask if it's not too gory.

I could go on and on, but I don't
chase glory.

Memento Mori.

03/10/19 00:39 Wage chainz

I don't want things I want freedom

It's been many days since there was a slave at least from what history tells us

But in this day and age you've got to pay your way food, water, shelter - freedom

We're said to be born free but we're just born wild and then into us is drilled the idea of a human

Yes you make a wage but you're still a financial slave, even a pension is a finite chain around your ankles

We all have restrictions and some of us privilege but just because I have more doesn't mean I see any less

Spare change for change fuck off
earn a wage why because you see
yourself as nowhere better off
surviving than them.

30/09/19 21:48 Week

Self-care Sundays

Mopey Mondays

Time to rethink my life
Tuesdays

Where did my life go
Wednesdays

This is for something bigger
Thursdays

Feeling achieved Friday's

Sanctimonious Saturdays are
for sleep

30/09/19 18:00 Cold noodz

I watched the wheat strands float aimlessly in the cold water pan

I told kat she needed to boil the water first

It will get hot she said

No shit sherlock but my wheaty threads shall now be soggy

Noodle floodle soggy woggy

I weep for I long a pot noodle

30/09/19 14:28 Stress

In my opinion

There's two types of depression

There's the runaway and the run anyway

There's those who have given up and those who are just always stuck

There's those that escape in a bottle, spliff, sniff, needle, pipe, pills

Then there's those who will do anything to stay away from that

Sure, everyone has highs and lows but those who get high have lower lows trust me I know

Sometimes I just think bout this world I can't fix I wish I could mend

but to no amends I'll ever come
close

So I'll just sit with my knees to my
chin hoping if I keep fighting one
day I'll win

Some even escape with a rope
because they've lost hope

There's two type of depression but
they're both the same with enough
compression it's just all a matter of
time before I resort to an escape
whatever mine will be

It isn't me that's sick, just that
some can better handle it.

28/09/19 02:26 Forgetting you

Lead awake

Thinking of you

Can't sleep

Thinking of you

When I dream

I dream of you

I wish I could walk away from my own thoughts like I thought I could walk away from your lies

But they follow me everywhere every step I'm under fire

I know you're drinking; your drugs and your fucks will make you feel your over me

But my solitude, my work, my poetry

Doesn't help me forget about you

25/09/19 21:49 Still healing, still broken

Healing means still broken

Wish that I had something to show for

Tell you that my way leads somewhere you want

But I still feel stuck, sad, sick, tired.

Let's call this an intermission

For I am not myself

I am myself but for the time being

I cannot be who you want

14/09/19 20:44 Lord

God is gracious

And a rapist

Praying to an idol

That impregnated a child

No wonder preachers think we
all want to sin

Heaven forbid

Those without faith in
themselves can only ever delve
into hope and belief of
unknown

How tragic for the masses that
they more likely sell their ass
to a church than believe in
themselves

You're told you want to sin by child raping priests all they are is following God's will

And all you are is damned from day one

12/09/19 19:55 Melancholia Warrior

I won't be another statistic

Even though my heads going ballistic

Sometimes you just grab the wrong end of the shit stick

If it weights me down I'll lift it

There's always someone who wants to kick it

Even a stranger, another outcast, misfit

Don't see my place in the world doesn't mean I won't fit

Stick the pieces of my mind back together with a prit stick

I'm in a dark place but I'll fix it

I'm on a long path but I'll stick
it

My mind is dark melanistic

Can't see the end of the road
won't have a bitch fit

I won't leave this journey cuz
I'm gonna beat it

10/09/19 00:47 No end

I don't see an end

To this bouncing around in my head without mend

I can't keep a friend

I don't see an end

Week after week I seem to seek a different means or dream

But my moods and my opinions change like the tide coming and going by each moon

I don't see an end

Some may say I can do everything, anything I set my mind to

But I can't set my mind

To

I can't sleep

Because whilst I'm awake I'm always trying to be upbeat and it's exhausting but in bed I then spend hours thinking about my next move

But there's no next move

I'm just running forwards with my eyes closed.

Or my eyes wide open and I can't move at all

I twitch a lot when no one's around to see, I scream, I shout, I cry, I hurt myself, but you'll only ever see me stood tall wearing a smile that you've seen before

I hate who I am I always have I hate who I've become even more

I hate what I've done all the people I have wronged all the loves that I have lost

I'm running out of reasons to stop myself from letting go

And when I say let go I don't mean I'm tense, but you'll know when I'm climbing up walls

I don't see an end

I've felt this way since 12 but it's only got worse with age

With each new option, risk, loss, decision I just seem to be walking to my grave

I don't see an end

I can't speak to my friends

Because I've already said it all before

And what does it help if I keep ending up back here

I don't see an end

September 2018 Moths

At least moths to a lamppost have ambition

Flying towards the sun like Icarus

But like we learned from Icarus

Fly to close to the sun

Get burned

Following your dreams

Will only melt your wings

Life isn't a climb

But an endless fall

We all end the same

Like the moth

Hitting the floor.

08/09/19 14:19
Different

I'm not different I'm not broken

Don't give me shit for being outspoken

You're just jealous I'm a showman

Better than you'll ever know man.

08/09/19 14:17 Netflix

What a sense of achievement

You attain from starting a new
season

Of a show that without you feel
bereaved

Sat on your ass

Letting time pass

Oh, what a great person you
are to be

07/09/19 22:47 Trouble

Trouble bubbles because ass
holes you don't know get to
make descions that affect your
life personally I think that we
shake hands look a past our
difference and show these
dragons that we hate them and
take the gold from beneath
their feet wouldn't it be neat a
defeat of the rich in the favour
of the poor for I am for this war
because I adore the sanctity of
life

07/09/19 22:44 Conflicted

Walking home

Sober and alone

The things I don't do for clarity

See everyone's addicted

It's a travesty

The masses unaware

Of the tragedy

That is war of mind

07/09/19 22:39 Blood

Did you know that your blood is thicker

Than all that liquor

That you're drinking

Every weekend

Drugs are drugs

Addicts have habits

Shun the pipe but not the glass

Bottle in a paper bag, do you know what you could have

And throw away

See every night ill have a
night cap but that's just to
help me sleep no peace for
the week

I just drink everyday

And that's okay that's fine

I'm following the law I fall in
line

But see this habit it's just
yours and not mine

05/09/19 00:44 Bucket

They told me don't do that you might die

I said what the hell else do you get out of life

See being born is a one-way ticket

Eventually the journey ends when you kick the bucket

Butt fuck it

There's lots to do on the in between

Think about everything that happens every minute

How many are born, see death, are sparred, how many people take a moment to care

The moment is everything it's in fact all we have

I'm gonna use mine recklessly alright lad

04/09/19 01:24 Shy breeze, autumn

When the wind shly sings

What does the cool breeze bring

The tips of my fingers sting

03/09/19 12:50 Laughter is medicine

In pain I laugh the burn that heals

Nothing, rain, sun they feel

02/09/19 17:33 Lie, alright

I like to lie,

I like to lie and say that I'm feeling alright

When in fact I feel like shite

Does that make me wrong rather than right

Because truth is I ain't lying from spite

It's so that you can keep feeling alright

And don't worry about my side

I can cry, my sorrow ill hide

Because I want you to feel alright

I'm okay

I lied

<u>02/09/19 14:13 Forlost</u>

My face, my name

You once knew

It's still the same

I haven't changed

Hear again

Here again

There again

Gone my friend

This isn't supposed to be how it ends

And in the end, you're still my friend

Talk

I don't wanna talk

But I miss your calls

I don't wanna talk

It never hurts less

I don't wanna talk

Because of what you said

I don't wanna talk

I wish I was dead

27/08/19 11:29 Cheat

Still don't get it,

Do you

Cheating can be done on a screen

But it's that fact that threw you

There's no touch,
no presence,
our exclusivity isn't compromised

Then why do you hide why do you lie

You see the touch of skin is purely that,

As physical as a bridge, a sunset, a hat.

But the conceptual boundaries you are crossing are the reason we both now feel loss and

You still don't fucking get it do you

There's no trust when you can't tell the truth

Start of September on a comedown; Woke

Pain ain't nothing but a feeling

I mean that sometimes we forget we're dreaming

Start, to lose, control of everything

Craziest shit happens whilst you're sleeping

A feeling coming deep from the inside of your meaning what it is to who are you where you going what you did

Just gotta keep rolling with the shit

Dropping in a hit

Getting up out that pit

Hit a wall smash it down

Pain is temporary but so is life
so why you giving up in strife
there's more to lose that hasn't
been anything that's already
never is

Again, but you carry on

Hit a wall smash it down

You only do if you're doing

Why'd you ever need to stop
moving

Cuz after all you're in a dream

We don't remember wake
whilst we're in sleep

<u>07/05/19 16:35 Morning</u>

Did I ever tell you you're still
cute in the morning

Did I ever tell you you're still
pretty when you're yawning

I don't even remember but the
thoughts only just dawning

Oh I wish I'd told you so

29/03/19 00:21 Vanity isn't profanity that's insanity

There's always someone:

Prettier

Smarter

Stronger

Faster

Richer

Taller

Smaller

Thinner

Thiccer

But there's only one me

And sometimes I'm funny

At times I have dimples at the right
angle with a certain smirk

If you think that self-love is vanity
that is absolute insanity this poem
in it has no profanity I'm just trying
to tell you to love you

Sometimes I feel like I'm not
interesting enough, like I'm trying
to impress this estranged primate
that I have nothing in common with
besides some dumb fucking meme,
is that all you mean? Because what
you see is what you get I'm not
making any threats when I'm direct
with you I'm just trying to be true

but all you can give me in return is
rehearsed nuances, scripted
procedure conversations and a look
that you practiced in the mirror

What you do

Where you from

Do you like cats or dogs

Like I actually give a duck

Tell me what you wanna be

Tell me your dreams and the ones
that you have no longer

Tell me what scares you what you
think about at night when you can't
sleep

When I ask you a question don't
think about the answer I'm not
telling you what I think you desire
I'm speaking from the heart and if
that's too much from the start then
please stop wasting my time with
your pretty eyes and Ha-Ha lies

I'm not seeking validation in fact
sometimes yes, I may want
attention, followed by a beautiful
laugh crack a smile and hey if we
talk a while maybe you should give
me your number

But you want me to impress
because of what society has
addressed toward you telling you
what you want

Do you know what you want? If not
don't tell me that's not what I've
got. That's fine. But I don't need the
confirmation that to you I don't
meet expectation. Have some
consideration for the man you just
looked down upon.

I'm trying to love me

If I'm not good enough for you it's
your problem not mine

I'm enough for me

You should be

22/03/19 00:47 Locked up if you speak up

Lock you up

Dose you up

So, you can't wake anyone up

I'm tired, trying to hold it
together at the end of my tether
I want to scream shout and
kill.

Just being honest can't you see
all the impoverished, the
famished, the maimed and the
mentally ill.

If you can hold your tongue,
and if you do truly care then
you can try all you can in your
career or your fam to make
little differences to your loved
ones' lives.

But is that enough? For me it's
all a bluff holding back what
you really want to do and say.
We can all see it, it's not even
difficult the system is fucked
our masters corrupt nobody
wants to carry on this way.

But they swallow their pride,
close their eyes and take a dive

I THINK WE SHOULD HANG
POLITICIANS BY THEIR
ANKLES

I am crazy, radical, an
extremist - don't listen to my
blasphemist words they will
only insight you to be a devil.
Despierta. Levanta..

22/03/19 00:34 Hate in the

I just want to be happy for other people

But all I see on social media is happy people

And it reminds me that I'm not

I try I really do try I try see love and give love everywhere

All I wish for is us all to be happy, loved and accepted.

But I can't even love or accept myself

When looking into others' lives, I think to myself

I'd like that, I want to do that but the steps I have already taken the path I have already made has set me far off from being where I truly want to be

So much time numbing the pain but never working toward making a name for myself.

I have things you want but it leaves me needing

I have things you need but I promise it's not what you want

I see talent and inspiration everywhere

But then I look in the mirror and see hate

21/03/19 00:01 Space wasteman

Don't wanna be a wasteman

I'll do all everything that I can

So that in the end I mattered

Because right now I'm a wasteman

When I was a kid wanted to be a spaceman

Now I'm here all I wanna do is what I can

To help you, and all, everything this

06/03/19 21:14 Cyclical

I never thought I'd fall in love

But yet here we are on my
wedding day

Wait not it isn't this is just
poetry

I'd rather have loved and lost
than to have never loved at all

Is a rather stupid phrase
because to not know pain or
even gain loves withdrawals

See I wouldn't like to have a
bike that got stolen

I'd prefer to never have a bike
at all

Cuz once I'd come off those
handle bars

My knees had been skinned
raw

As to a heart break

It's about exposing underneath

If you want to get somewhere

The pedals need be at your feet

01/03/19 19:53 I am alive

The feeling inside,

Reminds me I'm alive

And then that I don't want to be

Have you ever had an experience,

Something fearsome or fearless,

Something you remember everyday

Without fail

For me, I think about a lot of things

Why's it even matter

06/01/19 19:31 Geezer

Why can't you just leave a man
to drink

Sometimes I've got to think

And I'm flattered really it's true

But the truth is I don't really
want to talk to you

29/10/19 01:17 It needs to be said

It needs to be said

Every day more men, women and children are dead.

And I'm not talking about sickness, famine, casualty, or collateral of war

I'm talking about your family your friends your neighbours

I'm talking about suicide, and you should too

In fact, it should be so common subject it's no longer taboo

If I can make a joke in jest oh so macabre about this cigarette leaving cancer in my chest

Why not that losing my job, my partner a friend

Makes me feel as if I've no choice left

We need to talk about suicide

Because otherwise social rules get to decide

Which of my emotions I speak and I hide

Who I get to laugh with and who I can show that I cry

In school, in church in work in the pub

Tell your friends it's okay, give them your love

We need to talk about suicide because

Deciding your own fate is something nobody should.

06/11/19 17:39 Late stage capitalism

Sirens wailing

Privileged in Starbucks complaining

Societies failing

Dealers sailing

Children maiming

Snitches naming

There's no gold paving

Nurses in training

Armed pigs are raiding

Trauma we're trailing

Gods for nailing

Wasted life gaming

No gates just railings

The mad need saving

Satirically entertaining

Victim blaming

Kink shaming

Truthes get jailing

Wars of trading

Workers are slaving

In a thousand years is the
world really changing?

Filling time

Scrolling to fill the time

Is anyone else online

Life, don't know what I'm doing
with mine

Maybe looking for my piece of
sublime

From the universe a sign

Does this poem rhyme

Lemon and lime

Dirt and grime

Pineal like pine

Ugh here's another line

I feel fine.

19/11/19 13:01 Autumn

In my mind still, dead, dry

My room pills, bed, cry

Outside chill, shed, fine

In crowds, fill, dread, shy

Your head, thrill, said, lies

Fields, ill, lead, lime

Body will, red, time

29/10/19 15:23 Baby blue skies

The icey blue sky that I see almost tastes sweet when I look up to breathe it in.

That cold autumn breeze can take your breath make you wheeze stings my nostrils with much ease.

My fingers almost frozen so stiff they might as well be broken are you sure there's a hole in the ozone, bitter kisses on my finger tips.

I want to put into words the beauty of orange leaves for its the time of year when they flutter from seemingly dying trees.

Alas all I can now think is the fact we shed skin like trees leaves, bar the evergreens.

But even dust is beautiful in the right light.

05/11/19 18:09 Bin man

Today I met a good man

Today I met a proud man

Today I met a bin man

Who couldn't get the bus with his 20 pound note man

Got a bloody change receipt man

Kept a levelled head man

Sat with his cider can

Better luck tomorrow man

05/11/19 15:55 Forlorn thoughts

The dark days are bleak

Don't take my kindness as me being weak

I won't lose any sleep

Over someone externally extrovert that's internally meak

Don't you think it's peak

But every waking day your heart still beats

Underfoot of aristocrat cleets

Stand out get called a freak

Boring if you're not in the sheets

Cut the sheet

The wools over your eyes sheep

Watching Friends on repeat

Old gold lady won't kneel at her
feet

Old wooden lady mother at
sixteen, mother of three please
take my seat

Won't heave when the bus
smells like cheese cuz this is
where I be

Do I choose to know or be
happy

05/11/19 10:09 Coffee shop

Life is paid for in blood and sweat

The sweat on your brow is food in your mouth

The calisis on your hand is catharsis of hard earned pay

Brought to the world in blood sweat and shit

To live this life in blood sweat and shit

Praying for a better life is to never quit

The ache of your feet means that for another day your heart can beat

Who needs sleep with a coffee shop on every street

Each tear is a penny, drop of blood is pence your sweat is a pound it all sounds so profound

But this be the life we live

You're unclean if you're sick of it

05/11/19 20:20 Firework fawks

Bright lights

Smoke in the air

A time for us to forget our despair

Bonfires

Flashing whirling toys

Fun for the family the girls and the boys

06/11/19 12:26 Expectation

In your youth can't wait for responsibility

Now you've got it with added fear and insecurity

Told that you can't where you thought you could

Who'd ask for this nobody would

07/11/19 16:36 Confidence

I

Am not that confident

All though I'm told I have features to flaunt

But I still hear the words and names used to taunt

The younger me

I've been going to the gym for a year now, people say I look a lot bigger but that voice says yeah but you're still short, scrawny, ugly, stupid, dirt

Whys it so hard to set your own worth

As opposed to so easy to remember someone else's words

When I'm low yeah it does hurt

Man, I've been so low for so long I've
forgot how to flirt

I just keep buying tighter shirts

Hoping someone approaches me
and tells me some positive words

Isn't that narcissistically absurd

But still those other words

Those hurtful words

Those words that I had carved into
my skin

And when those depictions had
healed

I still had scars in my mind I
couldn't get rid

I'm still working on it

08/11/19 01:35 Salt

I could cry

But the tears just sting my eyes

I have the time

To make my life mine

I can hope one day somebody sings me sweet lullabies

As I die

08/11/19 15:09 Soothing Seasons

A breath of cool air as crisp as
the autumn leaves

Interrupted by the drag of a
cigarette inhaling a tiny bonfire

The awesome seasonal blue
sky seems as cold as the air

Unbeknown to office workers
sitting at their terminals in
despair

I am glad to be free as
terrifying as it may be

I get to witness the seasons as
they come to be

It's funny how we wear coats as the trees become bare

And the long dark nights we fill with food drinks and bright lights

As nature hides hibernating waiting for springs sight

09/11/19 01:06 Fidget

Hey, is it hot in here what just me?

Sorry sometimes I find it hard to hear

When there's lots of different noises here

Just by the shear fact I don't tell my brain which and which not to listen to

I hope I'm not twitching or flicking fidgeting itching sometimes I just find it really hard to keep still but I will if it makes YOU feel better ill just sit feeling like my blood is boiling maybe I'll even pretend you're not boring again I didn't pick the preferences my brain did.

12/11/19 00:45 I don't wish to know

How many false prophets want to profit off of pain

How many rogues will show a ruse to make us remain

How many teachers will teach us what they're told not what they know

How many liers will lay with us on our death beds

That I don't want to know

13/11/19 12:45 With love,

Hi,

I dreamt about you again

My imagination said we made friends

Funny how we could never come to those ends

But it's not really

I could try to make amends

But whatever I said you'd never accept

It's me it's me it's only me

It's all my fault

It was never we

Why'd I still care

I left!

I'm looking for you in the streets, on the bus in the pub the club

In puddles staring at my reflection tryna find the me that was in we

I know you'll have found someone else

You always did

But I did the opposite of what anyone told me

To get over you

I retracted into self growth, I haven't smoked
haven't sniffed haven't drunk haven't fucked

Nothing to make me numb

I'm just going to feel my way through

Still hope the best for you

As much as I hate you

I hope you're happy

13/11/19 16:02 Another shadow

I walk with no fear

Although through the valley of the shadow of death

For I am also a shadow

Of my deceased former self

13/11/19 16:02 Shadow

The opposite of shadow is
reflection

Both are from you projections

You have both from the
moment of conception

Both are sides of you without
imperfection

Nothing to Numb the feeling
nothing to Numb the pain
again again again again again

I dread to think, I dread, to
think.

Can't escape my own thoughts
no escape only face

I'd like to tell you about the brightside the side outside the one to look at

But I can't

I just keep going no matter what demon rears it's head and is showing I think I'm spiritually growing trying not to be moaning

But

14/11/19 15:08 Lone wolf

On this path to virtue I keep forgetting to remind myself it isn't happiness

I'm depressed

All I see around me is people going back on what they said

I'm trying to lead the good life and I'm going with the flow

It turns out trying to be whatever good is, is difficult to let others know

I walk the earth on my own

I'd rather this than be one in a group alone

14/11/19 16:24 Autumn sunset for Grandma

An opium high blue to an iridescent lilac

Plume pinks and juicey peaches

Are those grey or are they violet

An almost violently bright display

Purpost the raw beauty of nature

Autumn sunsets

Awesome

20/11/19 12:38 Cold cheek

My cheek is cold

Winter may be upon us

But that doesn't mean I don't
miss your warm embrace

Cheek to cheek

Face to face

You were a disgrace

So why do I feel the same

I left you

I had to

18/11/19 21:37 Monkey cage

We're all just monkeys in a cage

The walls we see in our society are a representative of our trees

Can't you feel the fact we bare our teeth as a means of conveying our fear

It's not that a smile anymore means this be mine here

But that before I showed you, I was terrified

Of these zoo walls around and my inherent demise

Is it any surprise that few glasses of ambrosia sends us into a rampage dragging our fists on the floor

Chest out, eyes wide, jaw low

Oo oo

We pick the best monkeys to rule over us, deciding which of our fruits to share and where our territory ends

And they spend most of their time flinging shit at one another making a mockery of our forest

They're cutting down the trees

And they're replacing them with machines

They're taking our fruit

And telling us to shoot our neighbour

I'll beat my chest but only in jest trying to express my desire for liberation

Give me the fruit I picked

And promise me my children will have trees

19/11/19 13:13 Bacon butty

Today I bought smack

Perhaps it was just a snack

To not would have been whack

In my veins do you see tracks

This man had but a sack

He asked to eat I gave him that

Is my distrust based on fact

Or knowledge at a lack

At least I'm safe from the blistering colds attack

Maybe a man ate maybe he smoked crack

19/11/19 10:16 Rock

I'm still finding

A comfortable silence

Where I don't have

To fill spaces

Just for bearable moments

There's no rocks

Only clouds of hot air

20/11/19 21:16 Lines in sand

Israel and palestine

Capturing your mind

Nobody picks sides

Racist or antisemite

Zionists or terrorists

Who do you side

Borders aren't real they're in your mind

And I'll think you'll find

The issue is bigger than who's land
How can a book draw lines in the sand

28/11/19 22:18

There's a man who picks
flowers

He doesn't pick them for
himself

There's a
man who
picks
flowers

Only ones
others
have left

There's a man who picks
flowers

For nobody at all

There's a man who picks the
flowers

Mourning people left on the
wall

There's a man who picks
flowers

Be he can't ever mourn

There's a man who picks
flowers

Making his hard-earned pay

There's a man who picks
flowers

And he can't leave any himself

There's a man who picks
flowers

Removing the signs of a tragic
death

<u>05/11/19 01:35 Authenticity</u>

It's hard to be authentic when I've got time to think typing letters on a screen

It's hard to be authentic when everyone is pretending this mood seems to be trending so I'll add to that dream

It's hard to be authentic when the world feels as though its ending why would I be me when I can be royalty

It's hard to be authentic everything's plastic non recyclable so doesn't real sound fallable

It's hard to be authentic isn't that tragic but what's fake is real is, is real is fake

Keep wanting the next iPhone because you're not worried about your next meal

05/12/19 16:35 Pied

It's at least nice to know you're still alive

Even after all of the lies

When our eyes met I could of cried

But I walked away then and I walked away now

Pied.

06/12/19 19:10 I'm not racist BUT

I'm not racist BUT...

The foundations and institutions on which I was raised and taught are

I'm not racist BUT

The media, police, politicians, celebrities, heads of schools and churches are

I'm not racist BUT

Thank fuck I don't have to myself put up with any of that stuff, and I commend anyone still here who does I wish you luck

I'm not racist BUT

If I get it wrong I may be ignorant but
please don't hold it against me I'm trying
my best to understand your pain were on
the same team this society around is built
up from the ground upon evil

I'm not racist BUT

I'd happily tear down this society if it
means equality

06/12/19 22:02 Baggage (Revised 27/10/21)

Baggage

Food comes in a bag, fruit comes in a bag, bread comes in a bag, wine comes in a bag, milk comes in a bag, water in a bag. Ice in a bag.

Clothes come in a bag, hats come in a bag, dvds come a bag, cds come in a bag (do cds come in a bag anymore?)

Shoes come in a bag, bags coming in bags, eyes come with bags, new squeeze comes with bags. Rake leaves into bags, kitchen cupboard filled with

bags, 10p for a bag, £1 lifer
bag.

At the shop with a bag
On a walk with a bag
At the gym with a bag
At the shop without mi bags

Baggage

11/12/19 12:46 Darkness Consumes

The darkness is coming
back

        Cut yourself

I came to see you in
weakness

        Kill yourself

I thought I would get
some catharsis

        You're nothing

But all it gave me was
this

You don't matter
You won't matter
Not to anybody
Spend life in misery
Your only salvation is
death

She says I can't
But I know I can
I've done it before
I'll do it again
In this alone
In till the end
Shattered psyche

Broken men
Star light heals
And so the moon
I'm still breathing
Looks like you lose.

Hello darkness my old
friend
I know we will meet
again
And again I shall
vanquish thee
Always now and till
infinity

Until the end

Darkness

My friend

On my final day

I shall see you again

11/12/19 13:55 Little Rain Cloud

Let me tell you about my love

Let me tell you about my dark cloud

Let me tell you of the fallen angel that sits atop my brow

She's makes my life misery but I couldn't live without

She makes the mornings heavy but the nights too short and the days so long

She makes me considerate by always asking what's right and what's wrong

There's times when she leaves
me and I think I can carry on

There's times when she leaves
me and there's nobody to tell
me I'm wrong

There's times when she leaves
me, but she always comes
back, she takes me by the
heart strings, and takes off my
crown, she drags me
underneath, I'll smile in the
face of death and with open
arms say

How long it has been little
rain cloud

12/12/19 22:34 Who we

We are what we eat what we do

what we want what we feel what we

touch what we see what we ear

what we smell what we taste what

we fuck what we preach what we

wear what we buy what we sell

what we fight what we lose what we

win what we prove what we search

what we find what we teach what

we ride where we live where we sit

where we go where we been where

we chill where we shop where we
stop where we sleep where we hide
where we hid where we cry where
we spit where we lied where we
swim who we are who we been who
we slept who we pied who we met
who we miss who we watch who we
listen who we follow we who mind
who we bother who we grip who we
love who we hit who we hold who
we kiss who we kill why we kill how
we live. We who.

16/12/19 22:56 Fuck this

Fuck the system, fuck this society, proud to be human I ain't proud of no nationality.

Fuck monarchs fuck bureaucracy don't like it get fucked by democracy.

Fuck roles, fuck gender fuck being a bread winner or sandwich maker.

Fuck race, fuck genetics your mother is my sister and it's all inherited.

Fuck war, fuck oil it's all just a facade and to the victor go the spoils.

Fuck faith, fuck religion, love thy neighbour but control is their ultimate mission.

Fuck illness, fuck "disability" why is human value based upon working capital.

Fuck sex, fuck sexuality fuck who you want, consensual and it doesn't matter to me.

Fuck global warming, fuck state lies care about the children but allowing them to die.

Fuck the rich, fuck poverty if this world is bottom up then who really deserves credibility.

Fuck you, fuck me too what are we doing here there's things we need to do.

<u>Shorts</u>

He sat awake

In wait

A message from her

He said

She said

They lied

In a superficial society
where does the value of
truth lie

If you never got to know
me don't pretend you do

(I'm) lonely but (I) hate people

When someone says they are fine they are not telling a lie but what they really mean is that they are alive... At least they are alive.

I write to forget

Yet here you are

I can't save you

I'll still wane for you

I just wanted to change you

Oh how wrong I was to

Three little words

When your eyes meet
there's

Viva la revolution

Tender love and care

Please like and share

Honey if you're after money

Don't look to me I just write poetry

Nobody there

Do you care

Give what I have to share

I would like some TLC

How selfish of me

To think of I before thee

The day was looking naff

Then I found a twix in
my bag

What is more human

To go against all odds

Or to give up

When the going gets
tough

Extreme words have
power

I love you

Cunt

Fuck you

Perfect

The gaze of others brings
us to our knees on earth
from the heavens

I'm getting too tired to
talk

I feel I've ran out of
things to say

Every conversation feels
like a hike

It's all effort I can't share

All I see is happy people
and happy faces
everywhere I see and all I
want is for them to be
happy I want to be
happy for you but I don't
have my own happiness
to give you any of mine

The sunset bled through
the black clouds

A colour of which I felt in
my souls eye

Filled with questions
awry

Mostly why

Respect all until
disrespect is needed

More friends more
funerals

We could talk about everything.

Instead, we talk about nothing.

@JustJonnyThings

@TheArtistEdie

#LookMumIWroteAPoetry
Book

Printed in Great Britain
by Amazon

85917479R00108